© Aladdin Books Ltd 1987

Designed and produced by
Aladdin Books Ltd
70 Old Compton Street
London W1

Design   David West
Children's Book Design
Editorial Planning   Clark Robinson Limited
Editor   Bibby Whittaker
Researcher   Cecilia Weston-Baker
Illustrated by   Ron Hayward Associates

EDITORIAL PANEL
The author Keith Lye, has worked
as an editor and lecturer on
geography in Great Britain, Africa
and the United States.

The educational consultant, Peter
Thwaites, is Head of Geography at
Windlesham House School in
Sussex.

The editorial consultant, John Clark,
has contributed to many
information and reference books.

First published in the
United States in 1987 by
Gloucester Press
387 Park Avenue South
New York, NY 10016

ISBN 0-531-17067-5

Library of Congress Catalog
Card Number: 87-80456

Printed in Belgium

TODAY'S WORLD

ASIA AND AUSTRALASIA

KEITH LYE

GLOUCESTER PRESS
London · New York · Toronto · Sydney

CONTENTS

How the maps work

This book has two main kinds of maps. Physical maps, such as that on pages 4 and 5, show what the land is like – indicating rivers (blue lines), mountain ranges (purple and dark brown), forests (dark green) and deserts (beige).

The red lines on the physical maps divide the regions which are dealt with in the individual chapters. Therefore, the shape of a region on the physical map corresponds to the shape of the region's political map.

The political maps, such as that on page 8, show the boundaries and names of all the countries in a region. Black squares indicate the location of the capital cities. Arranged around the maps are the flags of each country, together with the type of government, name of the capital city, population and land area.

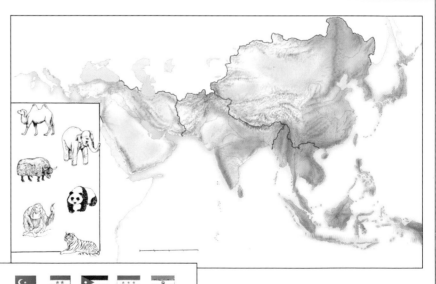

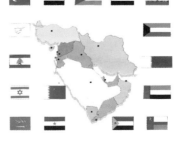

Animal panels

Alongside each physical map is an illustrated panel of animals which can be found in the corresponding region. Beneath each picture is the animal's common name, Latin name and the countries where it lives.

INTRODUCTION

This book is about Asia, excluding the USSR (Soviet Union), and Australasia, together with the Pacific islands. The USSR is partly in Asia and partly in Europe. In the "Today's World" series, the USSR is dealt with in the book on *Europe*. This is because seven out of every ten Soviet citizens live in the European part of the USSR. Turkey is also partly in Europe and partly in Asia. But because 97 per cent of Turkey is in Asia, it is dealt with in this book. The icy continent of Antarctica, south of Australia, is described in the book on *The Americas*.

Asia and Australasia contain a few rich, developed countries – namely Japan, Australia and New Zealand – as well as many developing countries. One of the ways experts measure a country's wealth is by its per capita gross national product (GNP). This is the total value of all goods and services produced by a country divided by its number of people. For example, the United States is a developed country. It had a per capita GNP of $15,490 in 1984. In the same year, India, a developing country, had a per capita GNP of only $260.

The Sydney Opera House in Australia

ASIA

Area: 27,606,800 sq km (10,659,000 sq miles), excluding the USSR.
Highest peak: Mount Everest, 8,848 m (29,028 ft).
Lowest point on land: Dead Sea shoreline, Israel, 400m (1,312 ft) below the level of the nearby Mediterranean Sea.
Longest river: Yangtze Kiang (or Chang Jiang); length: 6,300 km (3,915 miles).

Asia, excluding the Soviet Union, contains four main regions. *Southwest Asia* is largely desert, with rugged mountains in the north. *Southern Asia* is bounded on the north by the lofty Himalayan, Karakoram and Hindu Kush ranges. South of these mountains are fertile plains drained by rivers such as the Indus, Ganges and Brahmaputra.

The cold, dry interior of *Eastern Asia* is thinly populated. But the eastern parts of the region have moist, temperate climates – warm in the southeast and cold in the northeast. These areas contain some of the world's most crowded towns and cities. *Southeast Asia* is a tropical region, with mountains, steamy rain forests, densely populated plains and thousands of islands in the Pacific Ocean.

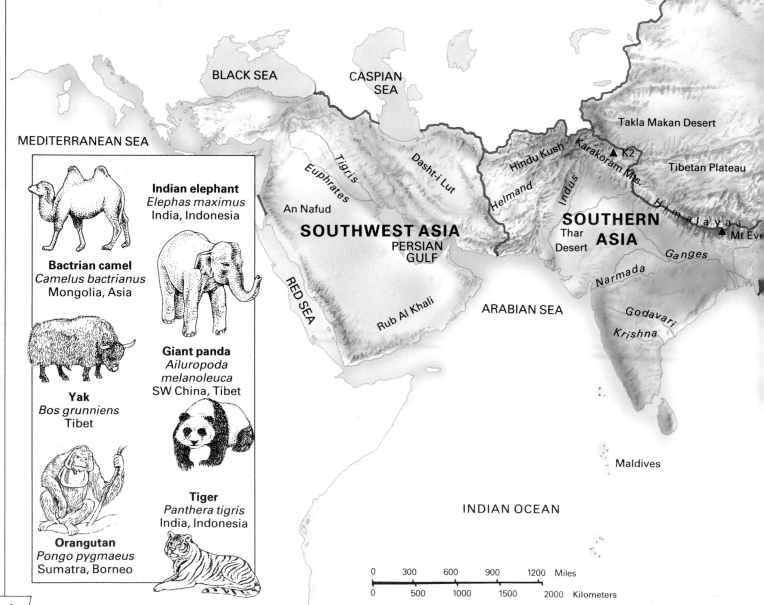

Bactrian camel
Camelus bactrianus
Mongolia, Asia

Indian elephant
Elephas maximus
India, Indonesia

Yak
Bos grunniens
Tibet

Giant panda
Ailuropoda melanoleuca
SW China, Tibet

Orangutan
Pongo pygmaeus
Sumatra, Borneo

Tiger
Panthera tigris
India, Indonesia

MEDITERRANEAN SEA
BLACK SEA
CASPIAN SEA
Takla Makan Desert
Tibetan Plateau
Tigris
Euphrates
Dasht-i Lut
Hindu Kush
Karakoram Mts.
K2
An Nafud
Helmand
Indus
SOUTHWEST ASIA
PERSIAN GULF
SOUTHERN ASIA
Thar Desert
Himalayas
Mt Ev
Ganges
RED SEA
Narmada
Rub Al Khali
ARABIAN SEA
Godavari
Krishna
Maldives
INDIAN OCEAN

| 0 | 300 | 600 | 900 | 1200 | Miles |
| 0 | 500 | 1000 | 1500 | 2000 | Kilometers |

Saudi Arabian desert, Southwest Asia

The Mediterranean coasts of Southwest Asia have hot, dry summers and mild, moist winters. But inland, hot deserts stretch from Arabia to India. Here, day temperatures often exceed 40°C (104°F), although nights are chilly. Asia also contains the cold Takla Makan and Gobi deserts, where temperatures of −40°C (−40°F) have been known.

Southern and Southeast Asia have dry winters with northerly winds. In spring the land heats up and moist air flows in from the south. This reversal of wind directions is called the monsoon. The southerly winds bring heavy rain.

Asia's high mountains have a polar climate. The windswept tablelands of Tibet, north of the Himalayas, have a subpolar climate.

Gobi Desert

EASTERN ASIA

Songhua Jiang

Hwang Ho

YELLOW SEA

Yangtze Kiang

EAST CHINA SEA

Xi Jiang

Salween

Mekong

SOUTH CHINA SEA

PACIFIC OCEAN

SOUTHEAST ASIA

JAVA SEA

Rain forest, Sumatra, Indonesia, Southeast Asia

Khumbu Valley, Himalayas

ASIAN PEOPLES

Population: 2,875,856,000.
Population density:
104 per sq km
(270 per sq mile).
Largest cities:

Tokyo, Japan	11,807,000
Shanghai, China	11,630,000
Calcutta, India	9,166,000
Peking (Beijing), China	
	9,020,000
Tehran, Iran	4,590,000

Asia has more people than any other continent and it contains the two countries with the world's biggest populations – China and India. It was the birthplace of several early civilizations – in the Tigris-Euphrates region in the southwest, in the Indus valley in what is now Pakistan, and in China. But much of Asia is still underdeveloped. Many people have low standards of living. For example, the people of Bangladesh, India and Pakistan live, on average, only 55 years. People in Western Europe, however, live, on average, 20 years longer.

Ethnic groups

The two main groups of people in Asia are members of the Caucasoid and Mongoloid subgroups of the human family.

Caucasoids live in Southwest Asia and most of Southern Asia. They include Turks, Arabs, Jews, Iranians, Afghans and most of the people in Pakistan, India and Bangladesh. The Veddoid people of southern India and Sri Lanka, however, are descended from an ancient group who lived in Asia before the Caucasoids. The Veddoids are short people, who may be related to the Australian Aborigines and to the Ainus, the first inhabitants of Japan.

Most Japanese (except for the Ainus who live mainly on Hokkaido), Koreans, Chinese, Tibetans and the majority of the people of Southeast Asia belong to the Mongoloid subgroup.

A few representatives of the third main subgroup of the human family – Negroids – are found in Indonesia, Malaysia and the Philippines. These are the pygmy-like Negritos.

Arab falconer (Caucasoid)

Chinese child (Mongoloid)

Languages

Many languages are spoken in Asia because the people come from a wide range of ethnic backgrounds. Major language families include the Semitic family (Arabic and Hebrew), the Indo-European family (Persian, Bengali and Hindustani), the Dravidian family (spoken in southern India and Sri Lanka), the Uralic and Altaic families (Turkish, Manchu, Mongol) and the Sino-Tibetan family (Chinese, Tibetan, Thai, Burmese). Japanese and Korean form a group of their own.

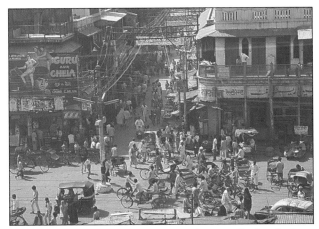

Over twenty languages are spoken in Delhi, India

Religion

The world's great religions – Buddhism, Christianity, Confucianism, Hinduism, Islam, Judaism, Shinto and Taoism – all began in Asia. Hinduism, Islam and Buddhism are now the main religions among Asian peoples. Religion has inspired much superb architecture. For example, the ruined city of Angkor was once the capital of a major Hindu-Buddhist kingdom in what is now Kampuchea. It was abandoned in the 15th century and rediscovered in the 1860s.

Angkor Wat, a ruined temple of the 1100s

Ways of life

More than three-fifths of Asia's people are farmers. Most of them farm small plots, largely by hand, and produce little more than they need to feed and clothe their families. When crops fail, the people starve. Many Asians are now moving to the cities, hoping to find work and better welfare services. But many become unemployed. Eastern Asia, excluding China, has the largest proportion of city dwellers. Although China has large cities, 78 per cent of its people live in rural areas. Many Asians have turned to communism in the hope that it will share wealth more evenly and raise their living standards.

Plowing near Canton, China

SOUTHWEST ASIA

Population: 160,913,000.
Area: 6,189,996 sq km
(2,389,971 sq miles).
Population density:
26 per sq km (67 per sq mile).
Economy: The average gross
national product per person in
1984 was $2,700. The poorest
country was South Yemen (per
capita GNP $430), the richest
Qatar ($27,000).

Southwest Asia, which is also called the Middle or Near East, is
Asia's most thinly populated region. It consists of 16 nations.
Of these, 14 are Muslim countries whose people are mostly
followers of Islam. In the other two, Cyprus and Israel, Muslims
form sizable minorities. Arabic is the chief language in 10
countries. In the others, the official languages are Greek and
Turkish in Cyprus, Persian or Farsi in Iran, Hebrew and Arabic in
Israel and Turkish in Turkey. Despite such unifying factors,
Southwest Asia is one of the world's most divided and
unstable regions.

Turkey
Republic
Cap: Ankara
Pop: 51,819,000
Area: 780,576 sq km
(301,382 sq miles)

Syria
Republic
Cap: Damascus
Pop: 10,931,000
Area: 185,180 sq km
(71,498 sq miles)

Jordan
Monarchy
Cap: Amman
Pop: 2,756,000
Area: 97,740 sq km
(37,738 sq miles)

Iraq
Republic
Cap: Baghdad
Pop: 16,019,000
Area: 434,924 sq km
(167,925 sq miles)

Iran
Islamic Republic
Cap: Tehran
Pop: 46,604,000
Area: 1,648,000 sq km
(636,296 sq miles)

Cyprus
Republic
Cap: Nicosia
Pop: 673,000
Area: 9,251 sq km
(3,572 sq miles)

Kuwait
Emirate
Cap: Kuwait
Pop: 1,771,000
Area: 17,818 sq km
(6,880 sq miles)

Lebanon
Republic
Cap: Beirut
Pop: 2,675,000
Area: 10,400 sq km
(4,015 sq miles)

Qatar
Emirate
Cap: Doha
Pop: 305,000
Area: 11,000 sq km
(4,247 sq miles)

Israel
Republic
Cap: Jerusalem
Pop: 4,208,000
Area: 20,770 sq km
(8,019 sq miles)

Bahrain
Emirate
Cap: Manama
Pop: 422,000
Area: 622 sq km
(240 sq miles)

United Arab Emirates
Federation
Cap: Abu Dhabi
Pop: 1,326,000
Area: 83,600 sq km
(32,278 sq miles)

Saudi Arabia
Monarchy
Cap: Riyadh
Pop: 11,519,000
Area: 2,149,690 sq km
(830,000 sq miles)

Yemen (Sana)
Republic
Cap: Sana
Pop: 6,339,000
Area: 195,000 sq km
(75,290 sq miles)

South Yemen
People's Democratic Republic
Cap: Aden
Pop: 2,275,000
Area: 332,968 sq km
(128,560 sq miles)

Oman
Sultanate
Cap: Muscat
Pop: 1,271,000
Area: 212,457 sq km
(82,030 sq miles)

Land and climate

Water is scarce in much of Southwest Asia. Farming is possible only around oases, in river valleys and on irrigated land. The Israelis are irrigating parts of the southern Negev desert with water piped from the rainier north. Oil-rich Arab countries, like Saudi Arabia, can afford to produce fresh water at desalination plants, where the salt is removed from sea water.

Turkey, the northernmost country in Southwest Asia, has a generally mild, moist climate. Its largest city, Istanbul, lies on the Bosphorus, a seaway separating Asia from Europe and linking the Mediterranean and Black seas.

The nearby island nation of Cyprus has a typical warm Mediterranean climate, making it a popular place with tourists.

Desalination plant in Saudi Arabia

Istanbul was once the Christian city Constantinople

People and way of life

Farming employs more than two out of every five Southwest Asians. Some nomadic herders live in tents and move around in search of pasture. Others live in villages consisting of mud houses. Farming in Israel is organized mainly through two structures: the *kibbutz* (or collective settlement) and the *moshav* (cooperative village). Some 90 per cent of Israelis, however, live in cities and towns. More than half of the people in Iran, Iraq, Jordan, Kuwait, Qatar, Saudi Arabia and the United Arab Emirates also live in urban areas. Urban life offers wider job opportunities, especially to women, who have traditionally had few rights in Muslim countries.

A Bedouin encampment in central Qatar

Culture

Jerusalem, Israel's capital, is a symbol of the complexity of Southwest Asia, being a sacred city for Jews, Christians and Muslims alike. Language and religious divisions also occur elsewhere. They led to the partition of Cyprus into Greek and Turkish areas in 1974-75, while many Kurds, a minority people in Iran, Iraq, Syria and Turkey, want to combine and have a country of their own.

The holiest city in Islam is Mecca, where the Prophet Muhammed was born. Islam now has two main branches, which differ about the succession to the leadership of Islam. Ayatollah Khomeini, who became leader of Iran in 1979, is a Shiite Muslim. Iraq's President is a Sunni Muslim. Religious differences and a border dispute caused the countries to go to war in 1980.

Orthodox church and Dome of the Rock, Jerusalem

Pilgrims at Mecca

Recent history of Palestine

For centuries, the Jews dreamed of returning to Israel, from which they had been driven more than 1,800 years ago. In 1948, Jewish settlers founded the modern State of Israel, but they were attacked by their Arab neighbors. A ceasefire was agreed in 1949, but further wars in 1956, 1967 and 1973 led Israel to gain territory: the Gaza Strip and Sinai peninsula from Egypt, the West Bank area from Jordan and the Golan Heights from Syria. Following a peace treaty in 1979, Israel returned the Sinai peninsula to Egypt. In the early 1980s, Israel invaded southern Lebanon to destroy bases of the Palestine Liberation Organization, which represents Arabs from Israel who want their own country. In the

Israeli forces, Golan Heights

early 1980s, civil war broke out between rival Lebanese religious groups. Apart from a "security zone" in the south, Israel withdrew in 1985.

LEBANON

The Golan Heights

SYRIA

Tel Aviv

The West Bank

Amman

Jerusalem

Dead Sea

JORDAN

Gaza Strip

ISRAEL

Economy

Southwest Asia's most valuable resources are oil and natural gas. The region contains more than half the world's oil reserves. Saudi Arabia is the world's third largest producer (after the USSR and the United States) and it is also the foremost oil exporter. Other oil-rich nations include Iran, Iraq, Kuwait, the United Arab Emirates (which had the world's highest gross national product per person in 1984), Qatar, Syria, Bahrain and Oman. Some of the income obtained from oil and gas sales has been spent on improving welfare and other social services. Other money is being used to expand the economies of the countries into other areas. However, the only developed nation in Southwest Asia is Israel, which exports not only farm products, but also manufactured goods such as chemicals, fertilizers and machinery. By contrast with the richer nations, the two Yemens are

A drilling rig in Bahrain

among the world's poorest places.

Wheat is the region's leading crop. Barley, maize, millet and rice are also grown, as are many vegetables. Fruits include dates, figs, oranges and grapes. Cotton, sugar beet and tobacco are also important products. Cattle are reared in the rainier parts of Southwest Asia, but camels, goats and sheep are more suited to the drier regions.

Construction in Saudi Arabia

Carpet-making in Isfahan, Iran

11

SOUTHERN ASIA

Population: 1,041,115,000.
Area: 5,136,733 sq km
(1,983,304 sq miles).
Population density:
203 per sq km
(525 per sq mile).
Economy: The gross national product per person in 1984 was $260, ranging from $462 in Maldives to only $130 in Bangladesh. This makes this region, on average, the poorest in Asia.

Southern Asia is the most densely populated part of Asia. It contains eight countries, which are all among the world's 30 poorest. Three of them – Bangladesh, India and Pakistan – once formed British India. When this huge territory gained its independence in 1947, it was torn apart by religion into Muslim Pakistan and a mainly Hindu India. Pakistan consisted of two separate parts: East and West Pakistan. Following a civil war in 1971, East Pakistan became the independent Republic of Bangladesh. Internal strife has also been a recent problem in Afghanistan and Sri Lanka.

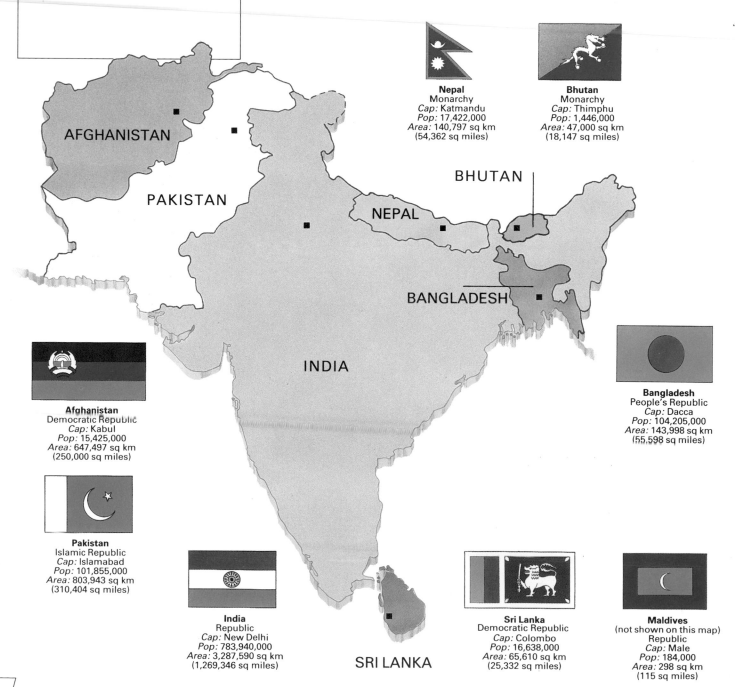

Nepal
Monarchy
Cap: Katmandu
Pop: 17,422,000
Area: 140,797 sq km
(54,362 sq miles)

Bhutan
Monarchy
Cap: Thimphu
Pop: 1,446,000
Area: 47,000 sq km
(18,147 sq miles)

BHUTAN

NEPAL

BANGLADESH

Afghanistan
Democratic Republic
Cap: Kabul
Pop: 15,425,000
Area: 647,497 sq km
(250,000 sq miles)

Bangladesh
People's Republic
Cap: Dacca
Pop: 104,205,000
Area: 143,998 sq km
(55,598 sq miles)

INDIA

Pakistan
Islamic Republic
Cap: Islamabad
Pop: 101,855,000
Area: 803,943 sq km
(310,404 sq miles)

AFGHANISTAN

PAKISTAN

India
Republic
Cap: New Delhi
Pop: 783,940,000
Area: 3,287,590 sq km
(1,269,346 sq miles)

SRI LANKA

Sri Lanka
Democratic Republic
Cap: Colombo
Pop: 16,638,000
Area: 65,610 sq km
(25,332 sq miles)

Maldives
(not shown on this map)
Republic
Cap: Male
Pop: 184,000
Area: 298 sq km
(115 sq miles)

Land and climate

The Himalayan and Karakoram mountains in Southern Asia form the world's highest range. They include Everest, on the Nepal-China border, and K2, the world's second highest peak at 8,611 m (28,250 ft), on the disputed border between northern India and China. The mountain kingdoms of Bhutan and Nepal are among the world's most scenic, and tourism is increasing. But life is hard in the higher areas, where winters are long and cold. In southern Bhutan and Nepal, the land merges into the lowlands of India, which are hot throughout the year, with heavy rain in summer when the southerly monsoon winds blow in from the sea. Some places have more than 500 cm (197 inches) of rain each year. The timing of the rain – which begins in April – is critical for agriculture.

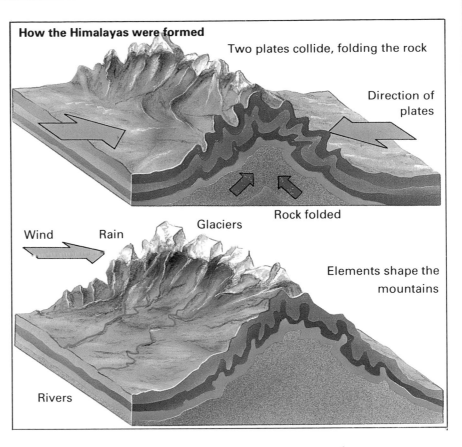

How the Himalayas were formed

Two plates collide, folding the rock

Direction of plates

Rock folded

Wind

Rain

Glaciers

Elements shape the mountains

Rivers

People and way of life

About seven out of every ten people in Southern Asia live in farming villages made up of huts built from mud and straw. Many people are desperately poor – India estimates that 200 million of its people live in poverty. Most of the area's cities are overcrowded and ringed by unhealthy slums. Many people have nowhere to live, and sleep in the streets. One of the region's biggest problems is its rapid population growth. For example, India's population increases by 17 million a year. This places a great strain on India's limited resources. Bhutan and Nepal are the poorest countries in Southern Asia.

A slum in Bombay, India

13

Culture

Religious and language differences divide the people of Southern Asia. There are also social divisions among Hindus based on the caste (class) system. Hindus make up about 83 per cent of India's population. Islam is the dominant religion in Afghanistan, Bangladesh, Pakistan and the Maldive Islands. Hinduism and Buddhism are the main religions in Bhutan and Nepal. Sri Lanka has Buddhists, Hindus, Christians and some Muslims. Religion has a great effect on everyday life in Southern Asia. Millions of Hindus visit temples along the banks of the Ganges and bathe in its water, which they regard as sacred with purifying and healing properties.

People bathing in the Ganges River at dawn, Varanasi, India

Recent history

Southern Asia has faced many problems in recent years, arising from poverty and also from religious, language, ethnic and political divisions. Religion splits India and Pakistan, and their borders – particularly in the state of Jammu and Kashmir – are disputed. India has many internal problems. Many Sikhs in the northwest want to found their own country and they have used terrorism to further their aims. Religious strife between Hindus and Muslims also broke out in the 1980s in the northeastern state of Assam.

Sri Lanka has also experienced violence, resulting from the desire of the minority Tamils, who are mainly Hindus, to form a separate state. They are opposed to the majority Buddhist Sinhalese. Political problems have led Afghanistan, Bangladesh and Pakistan to be ruled by military governments. Afghanistan was a monarchy until 1973, when army officers took over and made the country a republic. In 1978, a left-wing military government was formed. Many Muslims in rural areas opposed the government. In 1979, Soviet troops invaded Afghanistan to aid the government. But the Soviets were unable to defeat the Muslim guerrillas who believed that they were fighting a "holy war."

Afghan *Mujaheddin* (anti-Soviet freedom-fighters) in "safe house"

Economy

Apart from Afghanistan, where only about a fifth of the land can be farmed, and the Thar desert on the India-Pakistan border, Southern Asia has much fertile farmland. The leading food crops are wheat in the north and rice in the hotter south. Other major crops include cotton, jute, peanuts, sugar cane, tea and tobacco. Sheep, goats and camels are reared in the drier regions, while free-roaming cattle abound in places with abundant pasture. India has more than 180 million cattle – far more than any other nation. But Hindus regard them as sacred, and they are not used as food even when people are starving.

India has reserves of bauxite (aluminum ore), coal, iron ore and manganese. Pakistan has natural gas, and Sri Lanka produces precious stones, such as sapphires and rubies. Mining and manufacturing employ only 12 per cent of working people in Southern Asia. But manufacturing has increased substantially in Pakistan and India since they became independent. The leading industry in both countries is the manufacture of textiles. India has also developed heavy industries, including iron and steel works and factories making things such as cars, cement, locomotives and other products.

Jute growing in Bangladesh

Construction of a power plant, Bombay, India

Tea picking in Sri Lanka

15

EASTERN ASIA

Population: 1,258,179,000.
Area: 11,786,617 sq km
(4,550,839 sq miles).
Population density:
107 per sq km
(276 per sq mile).
Economy: The gross national product per person in 1984 was $1,430. This is the second highest for any region in Asia, and ranges from $10,200 in Japan to $330 in China. Japan is Asia's only truly industrialized economy and is its most prosperous nation.

Eastern Asia, which is also called the Far East, is Asia's largest region. It makes up more than two-fifths of Asia, excluding the Soviet Union. There are six independent nations. They include China, the world's most populous country; Japan, the world's third industrial power after the United States and the Soviet Union; and two small dependencies: British Hong Kong and Portuguese Macao on the south coast of China. This region is more affluent than Southern Asia. Its people live, on average, about 70 years, nearly as long as people in Western nations.

Hokkaido

Honshu

MONGOLIA

NORTH KOREA

JAPAN

SOUTH KOREA

Shikoku

Kyushu

CHINA

TAIWAN

MACAO

HONG KONG

Hong Kong
British dependency
Cap: Victoria
Pop: 5,465,000
Area: 1,045 sq km
(403 sq miles)

Macao
Portuguese Dependency
Cap: Lisbon, Portugal
Pop: 404,000
Area: 15.5 sq km
(2.6 sq miles)

Japan
Monarchy
Cap: Tokyo
Pop: 121,402,000
Area: 372,313 sq km
(143,751 sq miles)

Mongolia
People's Republic
Cap: Ulan Bator
Pop: 1,942,000
Area: 1,565,000 sq km
(604,250 sq miles)

China
People's Republic
Cap: Peking (Beijing)
Pop: 1,045,537,000
Area: 9,596,961 sq km
(3,705,408 sq miles)

North Korea
People's Republic
Cap: Pyongyang
Pop: 20,543,000
Area: 120,538 sq km
(46,540 sq miles)

South Korea
Republic
Cap: Seoul
Pop: 43,285,000
Area: 98,484 sq km
(38,025 sq miles)

Taiwan
Republic
Cap: Taipei
Pop: 19,601,000
Area: 32,260 sq km
(12,456 sq miles)

Land and climate

Eastern Asia is a region of contrasts. The rugged mountains and high tablelands of western China and Mongolia have cold winters and little rainfall. Parts of the northeast have an average annual rainfall of less than 10 cm (4 inches). The uplands and coasts of eastern China, Korea and Japan are much wetter. The rainfall ranges from about 60 cm (24 inches) a year in the northeast to 100-150 cm (39-59 inches) in central China and more than 200 cm (79 inches) in the tropical southeast. Average temperatures also increase from north to south. Most of the people in Eastern Asia live on the coastlands or in fertile valleys, such as those of the Hwang Ho (Huang He) and Yangtze Kiang (Chiang Jiang) rivers in China. Eastern China is sometimes hit by earthquakes. Japan often suffers from earthquakes and volcanic eruptions. It is a rugged country, with little level farmland. Japan also has a monsoon climate, though with slightly different wind directions than those further south in Asia.

Yangtze Kiang Valley, Szechwan Province, China

People and way of life

Apart from China, more than half of the people of Eastern Asia live in cities. In Japan, 76 per cent live in urban areas. The Japanese have adopted many Western practices. But while most wear Western clothes for business and other activities, *kimonos* (traditional robes) are often worn at home. Strong family ties and respect for authority are other features of the old Japan that remain important today.

Although China has about 30 cities with more than a million people each, 78 out of every 100 Chinese live in rural areas. Many live in communes (groups of villages where people work together). The Han, who are the true Chinese people, make up 94 per cent of the population. China has 55 minority groups, which include Kazakhs, Manchus, Miaos, Mongols, Tibetans, Uigurs, Yis and Zhuangs.

Traditional and Western styles are worn in Japan

Mongolian herdsman

Culture

China was the home of major early civilizations and the birthplace of two great religions: Taoism and Confucianism. In 1949, the Chinese communists proclaimed their country a People's Republic. Since then, religion has been discouraged and communist ideas have dominated, although anticommunists set up their own country on the island of Taiwan. The Chinese mainland government owns and controls all major industries, although some private enterprise is now allowed. By contrast, Japan followed private enterprise policies after its defeat in World War II. It is now a great industrial power. Politics has also divided Korea into the communist North and the anticommunist South.

Selling bacon in the market in Kunming, China

Recent history

Hong Kong Island has been ruled by Britain since 1842 and other areas were added to the territory in 1860 and 1898. Most people in this crowded territory are Chinese. They have made Hong Kong a prosperous financial, tourist and industrial center, with a thriving free enterprise economy.

Near Hong Kong is Macao, which has been under Portuguese rule since 1557. It is another tourist and industrial center, with an economy similar to Hong Kong's. Both territories have been useful to China, with which they trade. But Hong Kong will be returned to China in 1997 as will Macao in 1999.

Hong Kong

Economy

Farming employs about seven out of every ten people in China, which has much fertile farmland. China leads the world in wheat and rice production. It is also a leading producer of cotton, hemp, maize, millet, peanuts, potatoes, tea and tobacco. China has far more pigs than any other country — pork is the most popular meat — as well as millions of cattle, sheep and goats that are raised for food. Fishing is important, especially on inland fish farms. The country also has resources of minerals, such as coal, iron ore, tin, tungsten and some oil. Industry is well established in the northeast and is expanding elsewhere. But China's gross national product is low, being only $310 per person in 1984. In the same year, Japan's per capita GNP was $10,390.

Japan is short of farmland and it must import food and minerals.

The Bullet Train, Japan's high speed train

Yet it is a great industrial power, making cameras, computers, motor vehicles, ships and so on. Industry employs a third of the workforce. The chief food crop in Japan is rice. Sea fishing is a major activity. North Korea is rich in minerals and has many heavy industries. Farming is more important than industry in South Korea and Taiwan, but both are expanding their manufacturing industries. Mongolian farmers grow crops on collective farms.

JAPAN PRODUCTION OF MANUFACTURED GOODS	1960	1970	1980	World ranking (1980)
Cars	.17	3.6	8.4	2nd
Cement (tons)	22.5	57.2	87.8	2nd
Commercial vehicles	.6	2.1	3.5	1st
Merchant ships (gross tons)	1.7	10.5	4.2	1st
Motorcycles	1.5	2.9	4.5	1st
Radios	12.9	32.6	13.9	2nd
Steel (tons)	22.1	93.3	111.8	3rd
Televisions	3.6	13.8	14.4	1st

ALL FIGURES GIVEN ARE IN MILLIONS

SOUTHEAST ASIA

Population: 415,649,000.
Area: 4,493,481 sq km
(1,734,943 sq miles).
Population density:
92 per sq km
(240 per sq mile).
Economy: The gross national product per person in 1984 averaged $680, ranging from $7,300 in Brunei to only $180 in Burma.

Southeast Asia is a hot, wet region, consisting of a peninsula east of India and south of China and thousands of islands. Burma, Kampuchea (Cambodia), Laos, Thailand and Vietnam lie on the peninsula. Malaysia lies partly on the southern end of the peninsula and partly on the island of Borneo. Borneo also contains the small sultanate of Brunei, but most of this island is part of Indonesia. Other countries in Southeast Asia are the Philippines and Singapore, which became part of Malaysia in 1963, and then a separate republic in 1965.

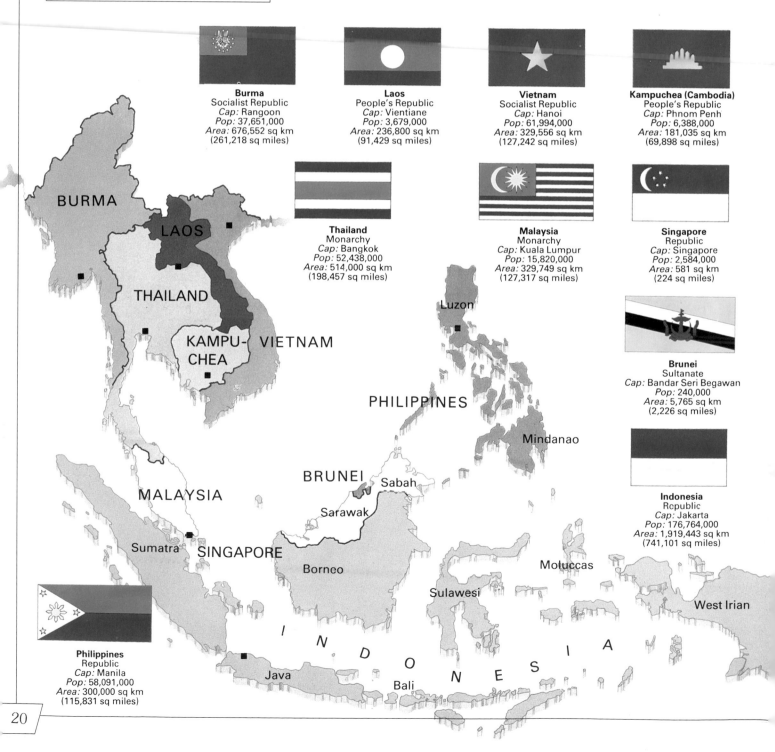

Burma
Socialist Republic
Cap: Rangoon
Pop: 37,651,000
Area: 676,552 sq km
(261,218 sq miles)

Laos
People's Republic
Cap: Vientiane
Pop: 3,679,000
Area: 236,800 sq km
(91,429 sq miles)

Vietnam
Socialist Republic
Cap: Hanoi
Pop: 61,994,000
Area: 329,556 sq km
(127,242 sq miles)

Kampuchea (Cambodia)
People's Republic
Cap: Phnom Penh
Pop: 6,388,000
Area: 181,035 sq km
(69,898 sq miles)

Thailand
Monarchy
Cap: Bangkok
Pop: 52,438,000
Area: 514,000 sq km
(198,457 sq miles)

Malaysia
Monarchy
Cap: Kuala Lumpur
Pop: 15,820,000
Area: 329,749 sq km
(127,317 sq miles)

Singapore
Republic
Cap: Singapore
Pop: 2,584,000
Area: 581 sq km
(224 sq miles)

Brunei
Sultanate
Cap: Bandar Seri Begawan
Pop: 240,000
Area: 5,765 sq km
(2,226 sq miles)

Indonesia
Republic
Cap: Jakarta
Pop: 176,764,000
Area: 1,919,443 sq km
(741,101 sq miles)

Philippines
Republic
Cap: Manila
Pop: 58,091,000
Area: 300,000 sq km
(115,831 sq miles)

BURMA
LAOS
THAILAND
KAMPU-CHEA
VIETNAM
Luzon
PHILIPPINES
Mindanao
BRUNEI
Sabah
Sarawak
MALAYSIA
Singapore SINGAPORE
Sumatra
Borneo
Moluccas
Sulawesi
West Irian
INDONESIA
Java
Bali

Land and climate

The mainland of Southeast Asia consists of forested mountains drained by large rivers. These include the Irrawaddy, Salween, Mekong and Red Rivers, which rise in China. The islands of Southeast Asia are also mountainous. Volcanoes are common. Indonesia has nearly 80 that have erupted in historic times. Fertile plains, fringed in places by mangrove swamps, border the coasts of most of the region. The equator passes through Indonesia in the south, and the climate there is hot and wet all year long. The northern part of Southeast Asia has a monsoon climate. Most of the rain comes between May and October. From June to December, there is a danger of violent tropical storms (typhoons).

An active 1,830 m (5,500 ft) volcano on Andonara Island, Indonesia

People and ways of life

The ancestors of most Southeast Asians originated in central Asia and China. They pushed many of the earlier Negroid inhabitants – Negritos – into remote areas. Later, Chinese and Indians settled in the region. Today, most people who play a major role in business are descended from these immigrants. But three out of four Southeast Asians live in rural areas, mostly in farming villages, in homes made of bamboo and wood. Many houses are built on stilts, which raise them above flood level. The region has some large cities, which are centers of government and commerce, with some manufacturing industries. The largest cities are Jakarta in Indonesia, Bangkok in Thailand, and Ho Chi Minh City in Vietnam.

A jungle village in Bali, Indonesia

Culture

Buddhism is the chief religion of Southeast Asia. It is the religion of Burma, Thailand, Kampuchea, Laos and Vietnam. However, the communist governments of the last three countries now officially discourage religious worship. Islam is the chief religion of Brunei, Indonesia and Malaysia. Indonesia is the fifth largest country in the world by population and is the world's leading Muslim nation. Christianity was introduced into the Philippines by the Spaniards, who ruled the islands from 1565 to 1898. Roman Catholics make up 83 per cent of the population. Singapore is a land of many religions. These include Buddhism; Confucianism and Taoism, which are followed by many Chinese; Hinduism, followed by the Indian population; Islam, the religion of the Malays; and Christianity. Southeast Asia has a wealth of superb religious architecture, including temples and shrines.

Jakarta National Mosque in Java, Indonesia

Recent history

Before World War II, Thailand was the only independent nation in Southeast Asia. The Philippines became independent peacefully in 1946, as did Burma in 1948. But fighting preceded Indonesia's independence in 1949, and a long war was fought for French Indochina, which was eventually divided into Cambodia (now Kampuchea), Laos and North and South Vietnam. A bitter war between communist North Vietnam and anticommunist South Vietnam ended in 1975, when the two were united under a communist government. Communists also took over Kampuchea and Laos in 1975. Communist forces were defeated in Malaysia in 1960, and an attempted communist coup in Indonesia was brutally put down in 1965. The region's last country to become independent was Brunei in 1984.

Local militia unit, Thanh Hoa, Vietnam

Economy

Southeast Asia is largely underdeveloped. Brunei has achieved some prosperity because of its large oil reserves, but the only developed country is Singapore, although it lacks nearly all resources. Its energetic and skillful people have turned their small homeland into a major industrial region, producing manufactured goods such as chemicals, electronic equipment, processed food, oil products, ships, and so on.

Most people in Southeast Asia are poor farmers, who use primitive farming methods and produce little more than they need to support their families. Rice is the main food and crop. Other crops are coffee, copra, cotton, palm oil, spices, sugar cane and tea. Forestry is important and the region produces most of the world's teak. Fishing is another major activity. Malaysia and Indonesia produce about a third of the world's tin. Vietnam mines coal, Burma and Thailand produce precious stones, while Brunei, Indonesia and Malaysia have oil and natural gas deposits. The cities have some manufacturing industries. A new source of income is tourism, with visitors coming from Australasia, Japan, the Americas and even as far away as Europe. Countries with growing tourist facilities include Indonesia, Malaysia, the Philippines, Singapore and Thailand.

A duck shepherd in Bali, Indonesia

Rice terrace in Banau, Luzon Island, Philippines

Religious architecture is one of Thailand's tourist attractions

AUSTRALASIA

Area: 8,510,000 sq km (3,285,730 sq miles).
Highest peak: Wilhelm in Papua New Guinea, 4,508 m (14,790 ft). Highest peak in Australia: Mt Kosciusko; in New Zealand: Mt Cook.
Lowest point: Lake Eyre, 12 m (39 ft) below sea level.
Longest river: Darling, south-east Australia, 2,740 km (1,703 miles) long.
Economy: Per capita GNPs range from $660 in Papua New Guinea to $11,172 in Australia.

Australia, the world's sixth largest country by area, is also a continent. Australasia is a term used by geographers for Australia, New Zealand and Papua New Guinea. These three countries are part of a larger region called Oceania, which includes the tens of thousands of islands in the Pacific Ocean, apart from those islands, such as Indonesia and Japan, which are in Asia. The islands of Oceania are shown on the map on page 33. There are three main island groups: Melanesia, Micronesia and Polynesia. Some are rugged, volcanic islands that have been thrust up out of the sea. Others are low lying and made mostly of coral.

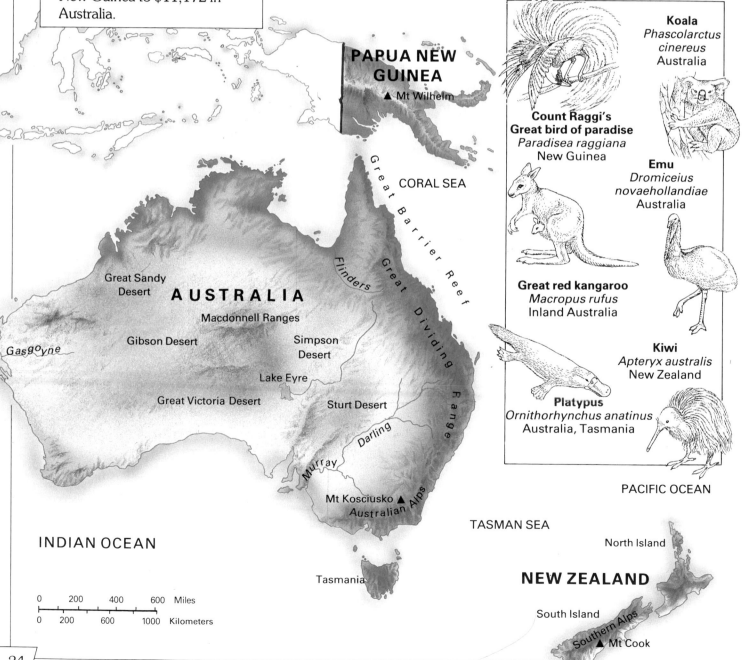

PAPUA NEW GUINEA
▲ Mt Wilhelm

CORAL SEA

Great Barrier Reef

Koala
Phascolarctus cinereus
Australia

Count Raggi's Great bird of paradise
Paradisea raggiana
New Guinea

Emu
Dromiceius novaehollandiae
Australia

Great red kangaroo
Macropus rufus
Inland Australia

Kiwi
Apteryx australis
New Zealand

Platypus
Ornithorhynchus anatinus
Australia, Tasmania

Great Sandy Desert

AUSTRALIA

Macdonnell Ranges

Gibson Desert

Simpson Desert

Gasgoyne

Lake Eyre

Great Victoria Desert

Sturt Desert

Flinders

Great Dividing Range

Darling

Murray

Mt Kosciusko ▲
Australian Alps

INDIAN OCEAN

Tasmania

TASMAN SEA

PACIFIC OCEAN

North Island

NEW ZEALAND

South Island

Southern Alps

▲ Mt Cook

| 0 | 200 | 400 | 600 | Miles |
| 0 | 200 | 600 | 1000 | Kilometers |

Climate and vegetation

The northern third of Australia lies in the tropics. It is hot throughout the year and has abundant rain. Mangrove swamps and tropical forests thrive near the coast, with savanna (tropical grassland) inland. The western plateau is dry and hot. Shrubs, coarse grass and stretches of red sand and bare rock cover large areas. The east-central plains are dry grassland. The seaward slopes of the Eastern Highlands contain tropical forest in the north and warm temperate forest in the south. Long periods of freezing temperatures occur only in the highest mountains and in Tasmania. Australia's 15,000 or more plant species include eucalyptus trees (called gum trees in Australia) and acacias (or wattles).

New Zealand has a mild, moist climate, with average temperatures higher in the volcanic North Island than in the South. Generally, the west is wetter than the east. Grassy pasture covers about half of the country and temperate forests another sixth, mainly in North Island.

Papua New Guinea has a wet, hot, tropical climate, although the interior is cooler and much wetter than the coast. The coastlands are swampy, and tropical forests blanket four-fifths of the land.

A desert in southern Australia

Mt Cook, South Island, New Zealand

Polynesian atoll

Urbanization: Australia, 86%; New Zealand, 83%; Papua New Guinea, 30%.
Health: Australia, 1 doctor per 500 people; New Zealand, 1 per 590 people; Papua New Guinea, 1 per 16,000 people.
Life expectancy: Australia, 76 years; New Zealand, 74; Papua New Guinea, 52.

Australia's first inhabitants were probably Aboriginal people who were pushed into Tasmania by the ancestors of the modern Australian Aborigines. It is known that the modern Aborigines were inhabiting the continent about 50,000 years ago. Poor treatment by settlers from Europe and the Australian mainland, who took their lands, and exposure to diseases against which they had no resistance, caused the Tasmanian Aborigines to become extinct by the 1880s. The population of Australian Aborigines also dropped from about 300,000 in the late 1700s to 70,000 in 1930, but numbers are now increasing.

Ethnic groups

The Australian Aborigines now number over 140,000, although many are of mixed Aboriginal and European descent. The Aborigines are often classed as a separate subgroup of the human family, alongside the Caucasoids, Mongoloids and Negroids. The first inhabitants of New Zealand, the Maoris, now number about 280,000. The Maoris are Polynesians – the name for people who live on the islands within the triangular area formed by New Zealand, Hawaii and Easter Island.

Polynesia is a term meaning "many islands." Some 98 per cent of the people of Papua New Guinea are Melanesians. This term means "black islands" and refers to the people of Papua New Guinea, the Solomon Islands and Fiji, who are dark-skinned. A third group of Pacific islanders are the Micronesians, who live on the small islands north of Melanesia. Micronesia means "little islands." The majority of people in Australasia, however, are of European descent.

Aborigine man, Australia

Maori mother and son, Polynesia

Languages

The British founded settlements in Australia in 1788 and in New Zealand in the early 1800s. Until World War II, most immigrants to Australia were British. But after 1945, only about half of the immigrants came from Britain. Others came from mainland Europe and, most recently, from Asia. English is the official language in Australia and New Zealand. It is also spoken in Papua New Guinea, along with about 700 local languages and Pidgin English.

Sydney Cove was made a penal settlement in 1788

Religion

The people of Oceania had a number of religions before Christianity became dominant in the 1800s. The huge stone statues on Easter Island in the southeastern Pacific Ocean are evidence of earlier cultures. They may have been carved in honor of the people's ancestors. Many local beliefs involve complex stories about the Earth's creation, gods and early heroes. Australian Aborigines believe that the past continues to exist in the present in what they call "Dreamtime."

Two of the 600 statues on Easter Island

Ways of life

Australia and New Zealand are prosperous countries. Most of the people live in cities and towns and they have high standards of living. Many of them enjoy an outdoor way of life whenever they are not working. But most Australian Aborigines have lower incomes than other Australians, although the government is working hard to improve services and job opportunities for the Aborigines. In New Zealand, most Maoris live in much the same way as other New Zealanders and they play an important part in society. By contrast, Papua New Guinea is a poor, developing country.

A beach scene in Fairy Bower, Sydney, Australia

Population: 24,900,000 (90 per cent of whom live in Australia, New Zealand and Papua New Guinea).
Population density: 3 per sq km (7.6 per sq mile).
Largest cities:

Sydney, Australia	3,333,000
Melbourne, Australia	2,865,000
Brisbane, Australia	1,138,000
Adelaide, Australia	969,000
Perth, Australia	969,000
Auckland, New Zealand	894,000

Australia and New Zealand became independent from Britain in 1901 and 1907 respectively. Both have kept strong ties with Britain, and the British monarch remains their Head of State. Papua New Guinea includes the eastern half of the island of New Guinea (the western half is part of Indonesia) and many smaller islands. In 1884, Germany took northeastern New Guinea and Britain colonized the southeast. Britain passed its colony to Australia in 1905. Australia took the northeast after Germany's defeat in World War I. Papua New Guinea became independent in 1975.

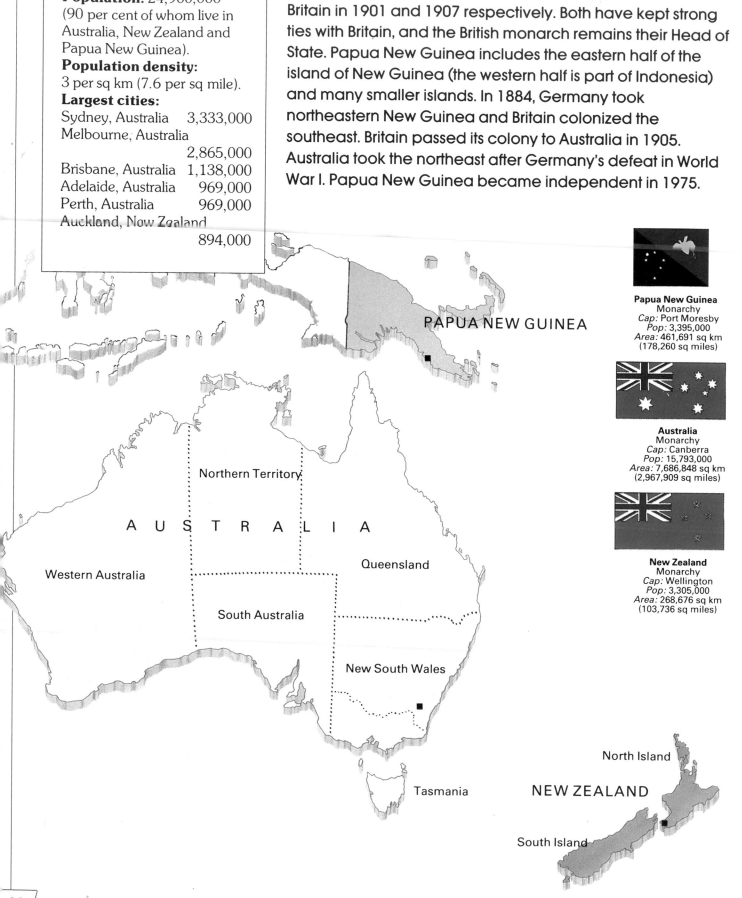

PAPUA NEW GUINEA

Papua New Guinea
Monarchy
Cap: Port Moresby
Pop: 3,395,000
Area: 461,691 sq km
(178,260 sq miles)

Australia
Monarchy
Cap: Canberra
Pop: 15,793,000
Area: 7,686,848 sq km
(2,967,909 sq miles)

New Zealand
Monarchy
Cap: Wellington
Pop: 3,305,000
Area: 268,676 sq km
(103,736 sq miles)

Northern Territory

A U S T R A L I A

Western Australia

Queensland

South Australia

New South Wales

North Island

Tasmania

NEW ZEALAND

South Island

Land and climate

Australia is an ancient landmass. Its mountains have been largely worn down and it is now the world's flattest continent. The mountain chain in the east is called the Great Dividing Range. To the west are the dry Central Plains, where farmers get water from artesian wells. The water originates as rain falling on the Great Dividing Range. It then seeps slowly through the rocks for hundreds of miles beneath the Central Plains. Australia's third land region, the dry Western Plateau, makes up two-thirds of this big country.

The North Island of New Zealand contains active volcanoes and many hot springs. The high Southern Alps form the backbone of South Island, and there are broad, fertile plains in the east.

Papua New Guinea is mountainous. Many smaller islands are volcanoes, and coral reefs are common. Coral is built up by tiny sea animals called polyps. The world's largest coral formation is the Great Barrier Reef off northeast Australia.

Geysers in Rotorua, North Island, New Zealand

The formation of a coral atoll

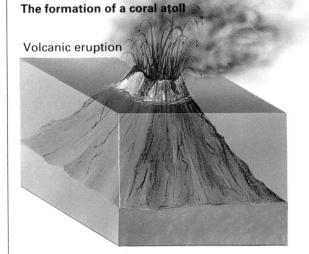

Volcanic eruption

Erupting volcano forms small island

Young volcanic island

Coral grows around new island

Sea and weather erode volcano crater

Coral atoll

Only coral remains visible

Coral islands

The first Europeans to make their homes in New Zealand included traders, hunters and missionaries. The Maoris, who had settled there hundreds of years earlier, called the newcomers *pakehas* (white people). By the mid-1800s, sheep had been introduced from Australia and farmers began to export wool. In 1861, a gold rush brought many adventurers to New Zealand. Only a few found gold, but many stayed on to become farmers. By the early 1900s, New Zealand had become a prosperous farming country and it exported large quantities of butter, cheese and meat to Britain. Manufacturing industries steadily increased in the cities, which grew in size. Today, manufacturing industries employ about three times as many New Zealanders as does farming.

New Zealand cut flowers being loaded for export

Ayers Rock in Northern Territory, Australia

Australians have become increasingly aware of the need for conservation, just like most people in Western countries. They have set up national parks and other reserves to protect wildlife, areas of great beauty and historic and cultural sites. One such place is Uluru National Park in central Australia. This park includes the high, red Ayers Rock, a major tourist attraction. Ayers Rock features in the religious myths of the Australian Aborigines, and cave paintings around the rock depict legends about their early ancestors. In 1985, the government handed over the title deeds to local Aborigines, who leased the area to the Australian National Parks and Wildlife Service for 99 years. This arrangement ensures that most of the money spent by tourists goes to benefit the Aborigines.

Culture

Cricket and rugby are among the most popular sports in Australia and New Zealand. They are also symbols of the fact that most people are of British ancestry. Ties with Britain have always been strong. But when Britain joined the Common Market (EEC) in 1973, Australia and New Zealand had to look for new markets for some of their exports. By the mid-1980s, both countries were trading more with Japan and the United States than with Britain. Many Australians favor ties with Britain through the Commonwealth, a loose association of 49 independent nations. But they also want to be part of a Pacific community, rather than an outpost of British culture.

Cricket is a reminder of Australia's British heritage

Recent history

Papua New Guinea contains a few people in remote areas whose way of life is still comparable with that of the Stone Age. Tribal loyalties are strong and tribal warfare still breaks out from time to time. But the country has been changing rapidly since 1975, when it became independent, and the government has encouraged economic development in order to modernize the country quickly. A major problem facing many small Pacific islands is that, while they want to be independent of foreign influences, they lack resources and enough educated people to create a modern, successful nation.

Tribal gathering in Papua New Guinea

Economy

Australia and New Zealand are developed countries. Australia is rich in minerals, which it exports. It leads the world in the production of bauxite (aluminum ore) and is a major producer of coal, copper, diamonds, gold, iron ore, lead, manganese, silver, tungsten, uranium and zinc. But manufacturing remains the most valuable activity. Manufactured goods include household items, iron and steel, paper, processed food, textiles and transport equipment. Farming is also important. Wheat and sugar cane are major crops, and millions of cattle and sheep are reared on the vast Central Plains.

Australia and New Zealand are among the world's top three producers of mutton and lamb meat and also of wool. Farming employs 11 per cent of New Zealand's workforce, as compared with 7 per cent in Australia. New Zealand exports dairy products, meat and wool. It also produces fruit, grains, tobacco and vegetables. The country has some minerals, including coal and ironsands, and its industries are varied. The chief manufacturing city is Auckland. Papua New Guinea is a developing nation. Farming employs 76 per cent of its workforce, but the country's chief resource is copper.

A natural gas factory in New Zealand

Mining coal in Yallourn, Victoria, Australia

Australian sheep station

PACIFIC ISLANDS

In Oceania, *Micronesia* includes the Marianas (including Guam), Palau, the Caroline Islands, the Marshall Islands, Nauru and Kiribati (formerly called the Gilbert Islands). Many of these have close links with the United States. *Melanesia* contains Papua New Guinea, the Solomon Islands, Vanuatu (formerly New Hebrides), New Caledonia and Fiji. *Polynesia* is made up of the islands in the eastern Pacific Ocean. It includes Hawaii, the 50th state of the United States, Tuvalu (formerly the Ellice Islands), Tonga, Western Samoa, French Polynesia, the Pitcairn Islands (one of which is called Pitcairn Island) and Easter Island.

Some islands in Oceania are mountains, often with active volcanoes. Others are atolls — ring- or horseshoe-shaped coral reefs enclosing a watery lagoon. The beauty of islands such as Fiji, Hawaii and Tahiti (in French Polynesia) attracts tourists. Hawaii has a thriving economy, but most other Pacific islands belong to the poorer developing world, where the chief occupation is farming. Copra (dried coconut and the source of coconut oil) is the chief product. Bananas, cocoa, coffee and sugar cane are also grown. English and French are the most widely spoken languages, but there are also hundreds of local languages.

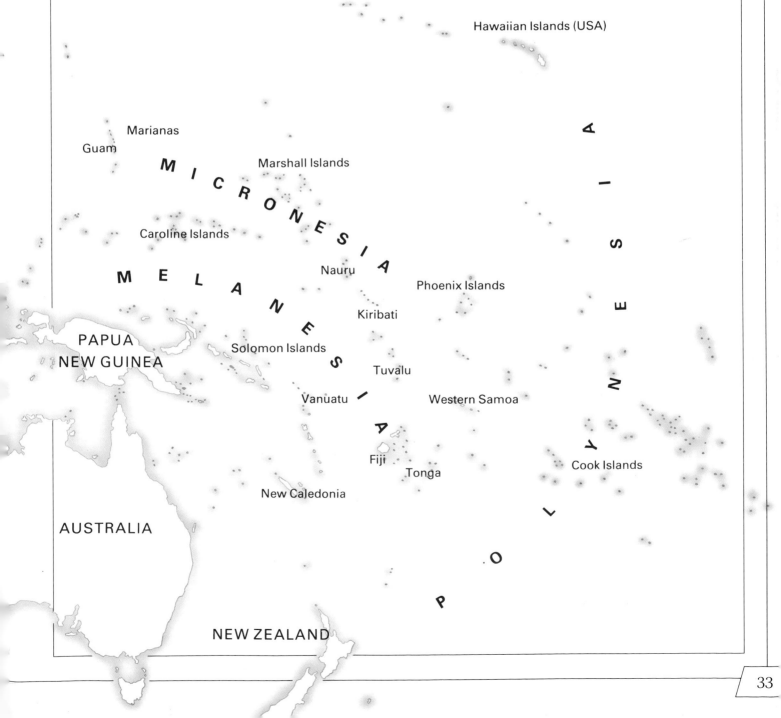

Hawaiian Islands (USA)

Marianas

Guam

MICRONESIA

Marshall Islands

Caroline Islands

Nauru

Phoenix Islands

MELANESIA

Kiribati

PAPUA NEW GUINEA

Solomon Islands

Tuvalu

Vanuatu

Western Samoa

POLYNESIA

Fiji

Tonga

Cook Islands

New Caledonia

AUSTRALIA

NEW ZEALAND

ORGANIZATIONS

Several international organizations work in Asia and Australasia. The Arab League, founded in 1945, consists of 20 Southwest Asian and North African nations and the Palestine Liberation Organization (PLO). Egypt was suspended in 1979 because of its peace treaty with Israel, which the Arab League opposed.

Oil-rich Arab nations, together with other oil-producing countries founded OPEC (Organization of Petroleum Exporting Countries) in 1960. They try to control oil production and prices to get more benefit from sales. They were successful when world demand for oil was high, but were less successful in the 1980s, when demand fell because of a world recession.

The Colombo Plan, founded in 1950, has 26 members. The rich members help the poorer ones by financing development projects. ANZUS is a defense alliance formed by Australia, New Zealand and the USA. In the mid-1980s, New Zealand banned nuclear-armed warships from its ports. The United States announced that the treaty was no longer in operation. But it continued military exercises with Australia.

OPEC delegates

ANZUS
Australia
USA

ARAB LEAGUE
Algeria
Bahrain
Djibouti
Iraq
Jordan
Kuwait
Lebanon
Lybia
Mauritania
Morocco
Oman
+ PLO
Qatar
Saudi Arabia
Somalia
Sudan
Syria
Tunisia
UAE
North Yemen
South Yemen

COLOMBO PLAN
Afghanistan
Australia
Bangladesh
Bhutan
Britain
Burma
Cambodia
Canada
Fiji
India
Indonesia
Iran
Japan
Laos
Malaysia
Maldives
Nepal
New Zealand
South Korea
Pakistan
Papua New Guinea
Philippines
Singapore
Sri Lanka
Thailand
USA

OPEC
Algeria
Ecuador
Gabon
Indonesia
Iran
Iraq
Kuwait
Libya
Nigeria
Qatar
Saudi Arabia
UAE
Venezuela

*Egypt suspended from Arab League in 1979

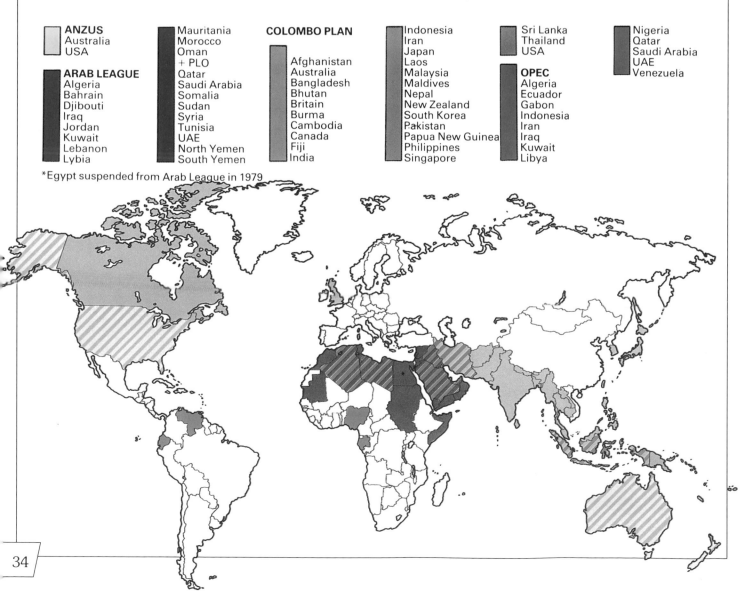

GLOSSARY

CLIMATE AND WEATHER

Drought Long period during which there is insufficient rainfall to support life and agriculture.

Hurricane Storm with very strong winds and heavy rain.

Mediterranean climate Like that around the Mediterranean Sea – hot, dry summers and warm, wet winters.

Monsoon climate Monsoon wind blows from the southwest from April to October, bringing torrential rain, and from the northeast the rest of the year.

Polar climate Very cold, as in the Arctic and Antarctic.

Temperate climate Lacking extremes of temperature.

Tropical climate Found close to the Equator – hot all year round with abundant rainfall.

ECONOMIC SYSTEMS

Capitalist Individuals own the means of production, land, factories, etc. and employ other people to work for them to produce goods and services at a profit.

Communist The state (the "people") owns and controls the means of production, in order to share more evenly the wealth created by their work.

ECONOMIC TERMS

Developed country One which is industrially and economically advanced.

Exports Goods sold outside the country in which they were produced.

Gross national product (GNP) The total value of all goods and services produced by a country (usually in a yr).

Imports Goods from one country brought into another to be sold.

Industrialized nation One which has well-developed industry as an important part of its economy.

Inflation Sudden rise in prices caused by availability of too much money.

Manufactured goods Made from raw materials or individual components either by hand or by machines.

Mass production Manufacture of goods (often identical) in large quantities, often on a production line.

Resources Materials that meet a need, e.g. iron ore to make steel, or good soil for growing crops.

Underdeveloped nation One which has not yet developed a high level of industry to support its economy.

ETHNIC GROUPS

Caucasoid Belonging to the group of "white-skinned" people; usually called "whites."

Mongoloid Belonging to the group of people characterized by yellowish skin, slanting eyes and dark hair.

Negroid Belonging to the group of dark-skinned people; usually called "blacks."

Pygmies Dwarf-like, dark-skinned people living in Africa or Asia (Negritos).

Veddoid From the Vedda (Veddah) people; ancient aboriginal race of Sri Lanka, now merged with modern Sinhalese people.

GEOGRAPHICAL TERMS

Coniferous forest Has cone-bearing trees (conifers).

Deciduous forest Has trees that lose their leaves in autumn.

Desert Region with little rainfall and few plants and animals; usually sandy. It may be either hot or cold.

Famine Severe lack of food usually caused by crop failure or drought.

Irrigation System of bringing water for agriculture from a place where it is plentiful to a place where it is scarce.

Peninsula Spur of land nearly surrounded by water.

Population density Average number of people living in a square kilometer (or mile), calculated by dividing the population of a country by its area.

Rural Based in the countryside rather than in the towns.

Savanna Land with grassy plains and few or no trees, often found between equatorial forests and hot deserts.

Tropical rainforest Forest in the tropics with trees that thrive on heavy rainfall; often called jungle.

Urban Based in towns rather than in the countryside.

Volcano Cone-shaped opening in the Earth's crust, through which molten rock (lava) comes to the surface.

RELIGIONS

Buddhism Founded in the 6th century BC, based on the teachings of Gautama Buddha. Practiced mainly in Asia.

Christianity Based on teachings of Jesus Christ and his followers. Practiced by Protestants, Roman Catholics etc.

Confucianism Beliefs based on the teachings of Confucious and his followers. Practiced mainly in China.

Hinduism Religious and social system, with belief in many gods, found mainly in India.

Islam Based on the teachings of Mohammed, practiced mainly among Arabs and Africans. Its followers are Muslims.

Judaism Based on the teachings of Moses. Its followers are called Jews.

Shinto Chief religion of Japan, based on ancestor and nature-god worship.

Taoism Chinese religion based on teachings of Lao Tzu.

TYPES OF GOVERNMENT AND POLITICAL TERMS

Colony Place settled by people who go to live there, but who remain citizens of their country of birth.

Coup Sudden seizure of power from an elected government by a group such as the military.

Emirate Country or territory ruled by an Emir (an Arabian prince, ruler or military commander).

Guerrillas Soldiers who are not part of a regular army but who harrass the enemy by surprise raids and sabotage.

Military government Sometimes unelected, supported by the force of the military.

Monarchy Government by a monarch (king or queen). In some, the power is limited, as in Britain or Sweden.

Republic Country in which the people elect the head of state and the government.

Sultanate Country ruled by a sultan (a Muslim ruler).

INDEX

All entries in bold are found in the Glossary

Photographic Credits:
(l=left, r=right, t=top, b=bottom, m=middle)
Cover, contents page and pages 5 (l and r), 6 (both), 7 (b),
9 (b), 11 (r), 13, 14 (t), 17 (l), 18 (both), 21 (b), 23 (t and m),
23 (t and l), 29 (t) and 30 (b): Spectrum; pages 5 (b), 7 (l
and r), 9 (r), 10 (t), 11 (t), 15 (l), 17 (t and r), 19, 23 (b), 25
(r), 26 (both), 27 (r), 31 (b) and 32 (rt): Zefa; pages 9 (l), 11
(l), 15 (t) and 22 (both): Hutchison Library; pages 10, 30
(t), 31 (t): Robert Harding; pages 10 (b), 14 (b), 21 (t) and
27 (b): The Research House; pages 27 (l) and 32 (rb): The
Australian Information Service; page 34: Rex Features.